Girl

Of The

Alamo

Girl

Of The

Alamo

For Cody Lynne Livingston.
"Remember the Alamo"
and Texas!
Rita Kerr
12-5-91

Rita Kerr

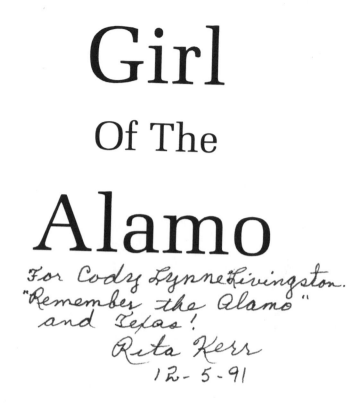

EAKIN PRESS
Austin, Texas

Girl of the Alamo

is dedicated to my husband,

Larry Kerr

Acknowledgments

Many people have been helpful in compiling the historical information contained in this book. Librarians of the various San Antonio public libraries supplied some of the books needed for this data. Thanks go to Charles J. Long, curator of the Alamo, and the DRT librarians Charline Pazliska, Sharon Crutchfield, and Bernice Strong. Authors Winifred Barnum Newman and Patricia Bigalow were also most helpful.

Special thanks go to history teacher Rebecca Churchill and her husband, Frank, for their suggestions and critique. Of course, without the encouragement of family and friends this book would not have been possible. Last, but not least, goes my heartfelt thanks to my husband for his research and advice in compiling *Girl of the Alamo*.

Table of Contents

The cry of Texas' freedom "Remember the Alamo" has echoed through the years. The legend of the heroic battle has been told and retold many times, many ways. This is the story of the only Anglo-American woman who was there. Susanna Dickinson lived those frightful thirteen days and saw the Texans go down one by one. Among those heroes was her husband, Almeron. Susanna's story is one of courage and strength.

It was the message that she carried to General Sam Houston after the fall of the Alamo that fanned the flames of liberty in the hearts of Texas patriots and led to their victory at the battle of San Jacinto.

1

Journey's End

"Squeak! Squeak!" Susanna mumbled to herself. For days that noise from the wheels had filled the air. Would the wagons never stop? Her body ached from bouncing on the hard wooden seat as they rolled along the rough paths. Usually walking was more comfortable, but a fine mist was now chilling the dismal February afternoon.

Pushing the wisps of hair from her brown eyes, Susanna Dickinson snuggled closer to her husband. "Try to get some sleep, Sue," he said, tucking the quilt around them as shelter from the dampness.

She closed her eyes and thought of her life. Sweet memories of her years as Susanna Wilkinson floated in her head. During her childhood on the Tennessee farm, there were many hardships. Life was a struggle in young America. Most schools of the early 1800s were attended only by boys from the well-to-do families. Susanna, like many pioneer girls, never learned to read or write. Instead, she learned the skills of a farm woman from her mother. Susanna was grateful. They expected life in Texas to be hard and cruel, too, with many difficulties.

A fleeting smile lighted her pretty face. She thought of her mother. How she had struggled to teach Susanna! She could hear her scold, "Now, Sue, you gotta learn to sew! You make those stitches smaller." Susanna wondered if she would ever see her family again.

Shivering from the chill that seeped into the wagon, she tucked her homespun dress and petticoats around her to keep out the cold. Pulling the cover to her chin, she thought of the first time she had ever seen Almeron Dickinson.

On that day in the blacksmith shop back in Tennessee, he had looked brave and handsome. His strong muscles had bulged as he hammered the redhot iron into shape. Shadows from the fire danced across his clean-shaven face. Bronzed by the summer's sun and blacksmith's glowing coals, his skin was like fine leather to her. She imagined she heard his soft Pennsylvania voice the first time he whispered, "Sue, sweet Sue."

Her mother teased that Almeron didn't have a chance after that. He became her Al. Serious and never wasting words, he listened to Susanna's chatter. He often said, "Sue, you talk enough for the two of us! You're as frisky as a high strung colt."

She could hear her father's joking, "Sue, someday you'll meet a fellow who'll take ya down a notch or two." And she had changed. She was just fifteen and he was twenty on May 24, 1829, in Bolivar, Tennessee. That day, almost two years ago, she started a new chapter in her life.

The first weeks of their marriage were spent in Bolivar, where Almeron met Green DeWitt and heard his talk of a place called Texas. Almeron listened and learned many things. He heard DeWitt say:

"Men, Texas is a huge place with acres and acres of unsettled land. It belongs to Mexico. Most Mexi-

2

cans live on the high, grassy area far from the woods and swamps. They raise sheep and cattle on ranches or *ranchos*. The government of Mexico wants to start Texas settlements in those areas not good for ranching. Mexico has agreed to give 4,428 acres of fertile land to every family. They would be allowed to live on the land for ten years without paying taxes. The settlers, or colonists, will pay a fee of thirty dollars and pledge allegiance to Mexico. Stephen Austin formed the first American colony. His group stopped between the Brazos and the Colorado rivers, and they named the settlement San Felipe de Austin." DeWitt paused, then continued.

"My grants give me six years to bring 400 families into Texas. They will settle 70 miles east of the Mexican town called San Antonio de Bexar."

Almeron listened. He decided—along with fifty-four other settlers — that they should go to Texas. Some families traveled by boat. Their group went by land. It was a slow, hard journey in wagons pulled by horses, mules, or oxen. There were few good roads. The paths and Indian trails grew worse with each turning wheel. Susanna learned to hate rain more than the plodding oxen. After a rain the rivers and creeks would rise, making crossings impossible until the water went down. Supplies got wet in the wagon. Mile after mile they shivered in their wet clothes. They traveled from twelve to fifteen miles a day in good weather, less in bad. Along the way the women and children searched for walnuts and pecans or roots and acorns to eat. The men hunted deer and rabbit but it was difficult to build a fire with wet wood. Cooking was a slow process. Memories of half-cooked meat and this rocking wagon these rainy weeks in this winter of 1830 made her shudder.

3

Day by day the landscape changed. The multi-colored soil turned from rich black to brick red to chocolate brown mud that stuck to the wheels like glue. The trees were every size and shape — from tall cypress along the creek banks to scrawny cedars on the rolling prairies.

For weeks Almeron made plans. He talked of land, of freedom, and dreamed of a new life in Texas. His words offered her courage, and gave her strength to overlook the cold. To help pass the time he taught her to load a rifle, and fire at a moving target. Secretly she hoped he wouldn't expect her to kill, or skin an animal. The thought of either made her weak.

Some of the luckier settlers had cows or pigs and sheep or chickens. Some had a dog or two, but since they hadn't been married long they didn't have much to bring. Almeron had loaded their wagon with his blacksmith and farm and carpenter tools. He bought sacks of seeds that served as pillows on rainy nights when they had to sleep inside the wagon.

The wagons, too, took a beating on the rocky trails. Often a wheel fell off, or an axle would need repair. Al was always eager to be of assistance. The travelers had started this trip as strangers, but now they were like one big family, sharing problems and troubles.

A sudden jar shook the wagon. Susanna was sure she would never forget this trip.

"Sue — , you awake?"

His voice brought her to reality. She rubbed her eyes and looked around. "Yes, why?"

"Look at those trees! This is good land, not too hilly and not too flat. That river over there — ," he

4

pointed to the clear, slow-moving stream near the trail, "should be good for fishing." She knew he was excited. "Sue, I think we're almost there!"

She studied the scene. "Oh! Almeron, are you sure?"

"They said this morning that we didn't have far to go. Look, the front wagon's stopping!"

Susanna watched the weary travelers climb from their wagons. Some patted the ground. "Good rich soil," a man yelled.

Crawling from the seat, Susanna's legs were stiff and wobbly. She couldn't believe the long trip was finally over. A few women and children raced to the river. "Looks clear enough to drink," one child hollered.

Susanna stretched her muscles, "What is today? I want to remember it."

"Today's February 20, 1831. It's a day we will all remember. The first thing we're supposed to do is sign some papers, come on."

Green DeWitt was standing on a tree stump as they pushed their way to the front. He exclaimed in a loud voice. "Folks, you've come a long way, but now you're home!" A happy cheer rose from the crowd. "This is Señor Ramon Musquiz, Commissioner of Mexico. He has certificates for you to sign. So line up, and after that you can select your site. You'll get your land title at a later time."

A deep voice from the back yelled, "I can't write."

"Me neither," someone called.

"Don't worry," Green replied. "If you can't write just make your mark."

The tree stump became a table for signing papers. Each man agreed to pledge allegiance to Mexico and wrote his name or made an X on the line. Susanna watched Almeron sign for them.

"Well, Sue, now we're Mexican citizens and can own 4,428 acres of Texas!" She stared at the paper. He laughed at her expression. "But, see, they spelled my name Almaron Dickerson instead of Almeron Dickinson."

She looked at the letters and couldn't tell what difference they made. He was the same to her either way.

"How about you women and children gathering wood for a fire and making some coffee, Sue? We'll go hunting. Gotta celebrate. Hey, DeWitt, what's the name of this place?"

"Gonzales," was his reply.

The name Gonzales sounded strange to Susanna, but she knew she could get used to anything after that wagon. The aroma of burning wood and roasting meat soon filled the air. The wind was cold without the sun's warmth, but Susanna didn't care. The journey had come to an end!

2

The Beginning

At dawn the next morning the excited families moved out to search for places on which to settle. Almeron selected a grassy knoll overlooking the river that was shaded by trees. The next job was to clear land for a homesite. The air was soon filled with the sounds of ax and saw.

Almeron chopped logs and notched each end with his ax so he could fit them together to form the cabin's sides. He used the oxen to pull the logs into place. Once the walls were up, he cut shingles for the roof. He placed a short-handled knife on top of a wooden block and hit the handle with a wooden mallet. The knife cut through the block and split it into a thin, flat shingle. The cedar shingles, or shakes, were fastened into place with a strip of bark from the logs. It was slow work.

Susanna packed river mud between cracks. The mud would seal the walls and keep out the cold wind and rain.

Almeron tied the last shingle into place and climbed down from the roof to survey their handiwork. "It isn't much, Sue, but it's the best we could get together in a hurry. Once the crops are in the ground and my blacksmith shop's built, we'll make a bigger place."

The one-room hut had a dirt floor and no windows, but after those months in the covered wagon she didn't care. "Almeron —, it's heaven to me."

Patting her arm gently, he said, "Still a couple of hours of daylight left. I'll work on a door. You could pack mud around the fireplace."

She looked at the wooden shape he had built in one wall. "Explain how this fireplace works."

"You'll pack mud and clay around this form," he demonstrated with his hands. "When it's dry it'll get hard. Flames from the fire will burn off any wood that isn't covered. If we need to repair a crack we just add more mud to the fireplace."

Susanna headed for the river with the buckets. "I see," she mumbled. Silently she hoped she did. Bucket after bucket of sticky mud covered the framework. While she packed mud, he split log planks for the door. He sharpened the end logs into points and fitted them into holes he cut at the top and bottom of the door frame. A leather string threaded through a hole in one log latched it shut.

It was dark when Almeron placed his tools in the wagon. "Sue, we've done a good day's work. Let's wash and eat that cold corn pone. You look tired. Tomorrow we'll move in, but for now let's bed down in the wagon again." She was too tired to protest.

It was good to stretch out for the night. They'd had a long day and worked hard. The wagon groaned as they settled on the soft feathered mattress, a wedding gift from Susanna's family. It was her prized possession.

The weeks that followed were busy. They plowed and planted the bean and corn seeds. Much of their future food depended on their work. Beans were important, but corn was a necessity. It meant bread, hominy, grits and lye for soap. On the trip, ground corn and water had been a nourishing part of their diet.

The warm spring days brought many changes around the cabin. Colorful wild flowers, many they had never seen before, filled the air with their delicate perfume. Susanna's favorite was a small blue and white flower the women called bluebonnets. Overhead they saw flocks of ducks and other birds flying north for the summer.

The riverbank contained many surprises. Often, at daybreak or dusk, they would hide in the thicket to watch the animals come to drink. Wobbly young fawns followed their mothers to the water's edge. Mask-faced raccoons washed their food before eating. Susanna discovered a rabbit's home at the base of a tree. The curious fluffy-tailed babies hopped about searching for food near their home.

May and June brought the hot Texas sun, but their work went on. One afternoon Al was cutting logs for his blacksmith shop and Susanna was working at his side. She thought to herself, "If my mother could see me putting this mud between these cracks, she'd think I was making mud pies!" Suddenly a sixth sense warned her of danger. She screamed! On a log in front of her was a diamondback rattlesnake! It lay coiled and ready to strike. It's tail rattled a warning and she froze in fright.

Almeron knew any sudden movement would cause the snake to strike. He eased his hand to his ax. Clasping the ax's handle tightly, he slowly raised it above his head. What if he missed and hit Susanna instead of the snake? Never had he known such fear! He aimed the ax and threw! He felt weak. The snake's body twisted and wriggled, it's head lay at her feet. He caught her in his arms as she slid toward the ground.

"Oh, Sue, I was afraid I'd miss it."

"I was too," she whispered hoarsely.

Almeron buried the poisonous head deep in the dirt. She watched him clean and stretch the skin to dry. Wiping his hands on the weeds, he said, "That was some snake! Wonder where it came from?" The question remained unanswered, and they returned to their work.

One of the most important chores each day was finding something to eat. The thicket around their cabin furnished juicy blackberries and grapes, as well as meat. Each animal Almeron killed was cleaned and the skin stretched tight to dry upon the ground.

Susanna kept two stones for grinding their meat. One day he asked, "Who taught you to do that?"

She replied with a smile, "My mother. She said the Indians taught the first settlers to grind berries and nuts with meat between stones like this. They rolled the meat and hung it to dry in the sun. That's what I'll do. Dried meat won't spoil. It will keep until we need it."

In the days that followed, Almeron kept an eye on the corn. The curious deer had discovered the tender stalks. Nosey rabbits around the plants became pests, too, but Almeron discouraged them by throwing rocks and sticks.

One morning Almeron took his gun and announced, "Sue, I filled your wash pot with water, and it's boiling. Think I'll go hunting for something for supper." He disappeared into the thicket.

Bending over the open fire she dropped lye soap

into the water, and poked the clothes into the blackened pot with a stick. The hot soapy water loosened the dirt, then she lifted them into cold rinse water and spread them over bushes by a tree to dry. Near her feet lay "Protection," her loaded rifle. After the snake, they both kept their guns ready.

Her back was to the thicket when she realized she was not alone. She grabbed the rifle and wheeled around. For an instant she froze. The wild-eyed bear was coming right toward her. She aimed and fired. The bear growled angrily and advanced. His hot breath touched her face. Susanna yelled and stumbled backward.

Almeron heard her scream and ran from the woods. He stopped. Before he could fire his gun, the animal's paw grazed Susanna's shoulder. She fired her gun. The bear fell at her feet. Almeron raced and caught her in his arms.

"You all right?" She nodded weakly. He touched the bear with his foot and saw the hole in it's chest. "Sue, you're some girl! You shot him dead!" Gently patting her arm, he added, "Bet you could outshoot any man in the settlement."

She mumbled softly, "Don't want to."

At supper that night Al declared. "A. J. Sowell has some work for me, but he hasn't any money. How would you like a cow?"

She exclaimed excitedly, "A real cow? That gives milk? We could have butter. Oh, Al, could we?"

He laughed. "Sure, a real live cow! And Sowell's dog had a litter of pups. Would you like one?" After the snake and the bear he secretly felt they needed a dog for protection. Frequently he saw strange, unfamiliar tracks down by the river. They needed a watch dog.

11

He grinned as he saw Susanna's face. "I'll get to that work real soon for A. J. We'll see about the dog."

A few days later Sowell and his boys came up the path with their unshod horses and broken tools for Al to mend. Behind them Susanna saw a brown cow and a scrawny half-grown pup.

A. J. called, "Howdy, Missus Susanna. Here's your hound."

She stared at the animal. It wasn't much to look at, but his sorrowful eyes melted her heart. She patted his black head as he licked her arm. "What's his name?" she asked.

"Don't have one. We have eight more so never got around to naming him. Cow's name is Flossy. Guess she won't care what you call her if you don't like that name. She doesn't give much milk. Maybe she'll have enough for you two."

The Sowell boys watched Susanna give the pup something to eat. The hungry dog bolted the food without bothering to chew. "He's sure a skinny thing. Think I'll call him J.B. That stands for Just Bones. Come on, J.B." She started to the river with her rifle and bucket. The dog followed right behind.

J.B. found his place in their family. He shadowed Almeron and learned to chase the animals that threatened the beans and corn. Each time he barked at an unfamiliar noise, Al would chuckle, "J.B.'s sure some watchdog."

After supper one night Almeron declared, "Sue, won't be long till that corn's ripe enough to pick. Sowell's offered to help me build a bigger house, then I'll help him when he's ready to build." He looked at the one-room cabin and continued. "We could put corn in here. Why this could be a barn for Flossy and the oxen when it turns cold!"

12

A teasing light danced in his eyes. "Would you like a house with a floor? And windows?"

"Windows?" she cried. "With glass?"

"Well," he shook his head sadly. "Windows but no glass. Have to make do with skins, sorry."

The next week they went to work. From dawn to dark the men were busy chopping trees. The chop-chop of axes shaping logs into lumber kept Susanna and J.B. company while she cooked their noonday meal.

When the final boards were cut, word went out for everyone around Gonzales to come to their house-raising on Saturday. Wagons started arriving before daybreak. The men brought axes and tools, the women brought food.

A soft September breeze cooled the air as the logs were rolled into place. The walls grew higher and higher. Stopping briefly under trees to rest and enjoy the midday meal, the group exchanged the latest news. When the men returned to work, the women and children gathered stones and rocks for the fireplace. The sun was setting when loud "hurrahs" proclaimed the walls and roof were up. Some friends started home to care for their animals and to do the nightly chores. Many stayed for the party and fiddle music.

It was very late when the last wagon disappeared into the darkness. Susanna remarked, "Isn't a house-raising a wonderful excuse to visit with old friends and offer a neighbor a helping hand?"

"Sure is," Almeron agreed with a yawn. "Tomorrow I'll cut holes for windows and doors. The last step will be the floors. Goodnight, Sue." She was already asleep.

Al's days were busy. Finally, sometime later, the house was finished!

"Sue, you ready to move in?"

She grinned, "I was ready to move in the day you started!" She made fast work of carrying her prized feather mattress and dishes to the new cabin. The big room was soon filled with warmth and cheer from a glowing fire.

After they moved in, Almeron thought of ways to make the cabin more comfortable. He drove pegs in the walls of the smaller room for hanging clothes. More pegs were placed above the fireplace for their two loaded rifles. He made shelves to hold grandmother Wilkinson's special pewter dishes.

The nights grew longer and colder. The short days passed quickly.

3

Changes

One morning a few weeks later, Andrew Sowell ran up the path. "Howdy. Pa sent me to tell you about Indians!"

Susanna yelled, "Indians?" Al stood waiting for his message.

Andrew continued. "Indians raided John Castleman's place. There's going to be a meeting at our house. I gotta tell the others." With that he was off down the path.

Almeron grabbed his gun and headed for the Sowell's. Susanna waited nervously for his return. She moaned when he told her later, "Some of us are going after those Indians. You and J.B. stay near the cabin till I get back."

He often bragged she could outshoot any fellow in Gonzales. He also knew she wouldn't kill a man, even an Indian. Thoughts of her husband chasing Indians filled her with terror. With her gun and dog at her side, she waited the long night. The next day she saw him coming up the trail. She raced to meet him. "You all right?"

"Sure, I'm fine. But we really had a chase. Finally got them on the other side of the river."

Settlers had other problems, too. Wild animals carried away pigs and killed the dogs. But Susanna's greatest fear was Indians. As Mexican citizens, the people asked the government for protection against them. Finally Commissioner Musquiz answered by sending them a cannon. Everyone was delighted and rushed to see it. Now they felt safe. As one of the town's gunsmiths, Al appreciated the six-pounder cannon and kept it shiny and ready. Susanna silently wondered if he didn't hope for another Indian raid so he could fire his precious brass cannon.

Months passed quickly. The Dickinsons had made many friends. Among them were Ramon and Francisca de Castenada Musquiz. They visited the Dickinson's home when they were in Gonzales and often invited them to San Antonio.

Christmas of 1834 came early to their home. Little Angelina Elizabeth was born on December 14. Little Angel was their pride and joy. Their lives were filled with laughter and happiness — until September, 1835. Then their life changed abruptly!

Five Mexican soldiers came riding into Gonzales. When the settlers heard them demand the return of the cannon, they were furious and refused to surrender it. Susanna watched eighteen men dig a hole and bury the cannon in a neighbor's peach orchard. A small army of more than one hundred Mexican soldiers rode up. Word spread through the colonies about the troubles they were having. Soon other Texans hurried to Gonzales to offer their assistance. The women stood nearby as their men dug up the cannon and readied it for firing. Someone yelled, "Let's gather pots and pans to beat into ammunition."

Another cried, "I can paint a picture of a cannon and write 'Come and Take it.' That could be a flag!"

The next morning 160 settlers armed with rifles

16

and the cannon exchanged shots with the Mexican force. One Mexican was killed and the others re-treated toward San Antonio. The first battle of the Texas Revolution had been fought, and won.

Later, the Texans bragged, "We won. That's the beginning of our fight for freedom from Mexico."

Some 500 Texans rode to Gonzales to plan what should be done about the cannon. After hours of talk, the settlers decided there wasn't much to do, but fight.

Almeron hurried home from the meeting to tell Susanna the news. "We're marching to San Antonio to drive out the Mexicans! Stephen Austin's been made leader of our group, and Austin has made me lieutenant in charge of artillery. I'll be back, Sue." He kissed his wife and baby. He was gone before she could protest.

Later, Gonzales received word that the Mexican General Cos surrendered San Antonio on December 9, 1835, after a short battle. The Mexican army agreed to leave. But it wasn't long before there were rumors that Mexico was gathering forces to fight again.

A few days before Christmas, Almeron, and oth-ers, came riding back to Gonzales. Susanna was thrilled. The baby was one year old and walking, and Al was home.

Then he announced. "Sue, I've joined the army to fight for freedom at the Alamo. There's going to be more trouble with Mexico. We left a small group in San Antonio, but I'm going back."

Before he could say another word she put her hands on her hips and declared angrily, "Almeron Dickinson! I'm not going to stay here alone! I won't

17

be by myself, not again. We're going with you!" He opened his mouth, but she went on. "If I'm a soldier's wife, then my place is with my husband!"

He stood there speechless. Then he laughed with a devilish twinkle in his eyes. "Sue, you're still as frisky as a colt! Wonder if you could stay with the Musquizs? Ramon and Francisca have always asked us to visit. Ramon is busy now that he's governor of Coahuila and Texas. Francisca might be glad to have you and the baby. Guess the Sowells would care for our animals until we get back."

He weakened. She knew he would. They bundled together a few things they could carry on horseback. With the oxen, the cow and J.B. they headed for their neighbor's place. The Sowells were happy to help their friends and the cause of Texas.

The family watched them ride off toward San Antonio. Susanna sat behind Almeron holding the baby in her arms. She was torn with excitement, fear, and dread. This journey was not a nightmare like the wagon trip.

San Antonio was almost a fairyland to Susanna after the handful of homes in Gonzales. Almeron pointed out the two Spanish missions: San Jose with its beautiful Rose Window and Mission Concepcion with its twin towers. Susanna cried, "Oh, how beautiful." Her eyes were round with wonder.

They found the flat-roofed Musquiz home without trouble. Everyone knew the governor. Ramon and Francisca were surprised to see them and welcomed them with open arms. The Musquiz home, with its beautiful flowers, became their own special quarters on the Main Plaza, or Square. Almeron had been right; Ramon was often away in Coahuila and Francisca was left alone. She was grateful for their company.

Life in San Antonio was different from any Susanna had ever known. The river twisted through the town and furnished their water. Washdays found the women along the banks slapping clothes with flat stones to loosen the dirt. The drying garments hanging on the bushes looked like flowers to Susanna. On afternoon walks she saw the poor wooden shacks, or *jacals,* and the high walls that concealed the wealthy Veramendi home.

The luxurious Musquiz *hacienda* of mud-dried adobe became their home. Francisca declared often, *"Mi casa es su casa,* my house is your house."

One morning Susanna looked at her friend and said, "Oh, Francisca, you are so sweet to us, and you are so beautiful with your long black hair and flashing eyes." She looked at her own homespun dress. "I'm just a country girl."

With a smile on her face, Señora Musquiz answered, "You wait here." She left the room and soon returned with her hands full. She combed Susanna's long hair into two braids and placed a red flower from her garden behind Susanna's ear. Around her shoulders Francisca placed her own colorful Mexican shawl she wore to church. "There," she exclaimed happily, *"Tú eres hermosa,* you are lovely."

Later, Al teased her. "I married a Tennessee babe; now she's my Texas girl!"

She knew he was proud, for he introduced her to everyone. He invited his special friend, Dr. John Sutherland, to share their home. Later Davy Crockett and David Cummings came to stay.

Susanna liked backwoodsman Davy Crockett; he reminded her of her father. His slow Tennessee drawl made her homesick. He fell in love with their daughter! Six-foot Davy would take Angie in his

19

arms at bedtime and sing her to sleep. He enlivened their evening with tales of alligator rides and Indian fights. Susanna thought Davy was gentle and kind.

Angelina was her mother's shadow. When Susanna cooked or worked, the baby toddled right behind. Life in the Musquiz home centered around their angel. Her dark, sparkling eyes, dimpled cheeks and precious ways, drove away thoughts of war, and the advancing of Santa Anna's Mexican army. But more and more Susanna heard talk of fighting and trouble with Mexico. Fears of war were squeezing out her happiness like a cold icy hand.

Each day Almeron went to the Alamo to ready the eighteen old cannons for fighting. Susanna knew the Alamo was very special to the people. After their arrival in San Antonio, Francisca had told her the history of the church. She explained how the Spanish priests had come to Texas in 1718 to teach the Indians. Together they built the three-foot-thick walls to enclose the three acres of land. They lived in small adobe rooms along three of the walls. One of the two buildings was a two-story mission convent. The incompleted mission or church was called San Antonio de Valero. The place was later called "Alamo" because soldiers from Alamo del Parras, Coahuila had used the abandoned mission in later years as barracks.

The priests taught the Indians to plant and work the land. They dug ditches to irrigate their crops. But the restless Indians returned to their old ways and left the mission. It had been abandoned for years. Parts of the roof collapsed, making it impossible to hold religious services. The mission was half a mile from the town of San Antonio de Bexar.

For two months they were happy in San Antonio, then it all came to a crashing end!

Susanna was telling Francisca, "Today is February 23, 1836, and, — " She stopped. From across the plaza the bells of San Fernando Church suddenly began to ring. Francisca clutched the shawl around her shoulders and dashed into the street to learn the meaning of the bells.

She returned crying and moaning, "Oh, Sue, General Santa Anna's army has been seen by the lookout. His troops are not far away." As officials of the Mexican government, the Musquiz family was secure, but they were concerned for their friends. "Let me carry Angie while you get your things. You must take these blankets on the bed for the baby."

Susanna groaned, "What should I do? Where is Al?" Suddenly she heard the sound of a galloping horse and, running to the door, she saw her husband pull his horse to a stop at the door.

"Give me the baby," he cried. "Jump up behind me — ask no questions." Susanna only had time to wave and throw a kiss to Francisca before they were off!

What a wild ride they had! Excited people were running from their homes, loaded with all they could carry. They filled the narrow streets with confusion. Almeron avoided the madness of the main streets and bridges to take them into the Alamo. Once inside, they found more confusion. The once quiet churchyard was alive with activity.

Cannons were being moved into place along the Alamo walls. Men were breaking lead and metal for ammunition. Susan recognized Green Jameson among them. Almeron hurried into a side room of the church with his family. "Sue, I need to see what

I can do," Al said. Susanna helped wherever she could. She loaded rifles and carried water. She saw the men carrying blankets, guns, and supplies inside the walls. From the huts and fields nearby they found eighty bushels of dried corn and thirty head of cattle.

During the confusion Jim Bowie collapsed and was taken to a room near the chapel. "Mrs. Dickinson, can you look after him?" someone called. Susanna bathed his feverish face. He had looked sick for weeks. Some whispered James had pneumonia, others tuberculosis or typhoid.

Bowie was a legend. Susanna knew the wildest and toughest men respected Jim and his giant, single-edged steel bowie knife. There were many stories about how he had come to Texas to hunt for the lost San Saba silver mines but found a wife instead. He had fallen in love with beautiful Ursula Veramendi and married her. After that, Jim became a wealthy, honored citizen of San Antonio. He let his beloved wife and two small children go to Mexico to visit her parents, and while they were there they became ill with cholera and all three died, along with Ursula's parents. Everyone knew Jim was brokenhearted. The excitement for life was gone from him. He had fought with the Texans last year to drive out the Mexican army and was ready to fight again. But before the fighting could start he had given his command to William Travis, because of his illness.

The long day, February 23, 1836, came to an end. Susanna was tired and frightened as she lay on the cot beside Angelina. From the adjoining chapel came muffled sobs and prayers of the Mexican women and children. They, too, were afraid of Santa Anna's army. Susanna knew that among them were

22

Francisca's friends, Anna Esparza and her four children as well as pretty Trinidad Saucedo.

Susanna looked at the pale light coming from the lone window high above the bed. She was sure the mission walls were still strong, but could they withstand bombardment from cannon?

The night's stillness was shaken. Susanna sat up and listened. Across the way the Mexican band blared a rousing song. The noise of drums and bugles filled the darkness. Then silence! The band stopped as suddenly as it had started.

Now, Susanna realized, there was something more dreadful than snakes or Indians; there was Santa Anna. Santa Anna, cruel and arrogant in his headquarters in the Yturri home on Main Plaza couldn't know that even his name made her tremble — General Antonio Lopez de Santa Anna!

4

Fear Creeps In

"It was a noisy night, wasn't it, Al?" Susanna said the next morning.

"Some of it was when Albert Martin left. Understand he took a message from Colonel Travis to Gonzales. Part of Travis's letter said:

> To the People of Texas and All Americans in the world . . . I have sustained a continual bombardment and cannonade for 24 hours and have not lost a man . . . I shall never surrender or retreat . . . Victory or Death!

Almeron's voice was serious. "There may be heavy shooting, Sue. If you come out to help, you be careful. Davy says that red flag on San Fernando means 'no quarter,' no prisoners will be taken. It'll mean a fight to the death." His voice faltered. "You know Dr. Sutherland and John Smith left yesterday for Gonzales to ask for help. No telling when it'll come. Wish you and the baby were back home. You'd be safe there."

She said softly, "Now, Al, you know I'm a soldier's wife and Angelina's a soldier's baby. Our place is here with you."

He looked into her eyes and touched her long hair coiled in a bun on her neck. "I know. Guess I'd better get back to the roof."

Susanna saw Green Jameson checking the weak spot in the wall between the low barracks and the church. Dirt braced the wooden boards that would act as a shield when the fighting started. That post was assigned to Crockett and his twelve Tennesseans.

Susanna joined the women near the fire. Kneeling on the ground, they patted balls of ground corn moistened with water into thin round shapes called tortillas. These were browned in a flat skillet, then filled with peppered beans. The two Negro servants, Joe and Sam, took them to the hungry men around the wall. Enrique, the oldest Esparza child, carried breakfast to the other children.

Throughout the morning of February 24 the air was clouded with smoke. Inside the chapel the minutes and hours passed slowly. To the frightened group the dreadful noise of battle was never ending. Suddenly, Mexican bugles blared from outside the wall. Al yelled from the roof, "Watch those huts, boys."

Davy fired a warning shot with "Betsy," his rifle. Guns from the church roof blended with musket fire. Susanna crawled to the church door and peeked out. Through the haze she saw two men, crouched near the ground, slipping out the south gate. Soon black smoke bellowed into the sky. When they returned Susanna recognized James Rose. He yelled, "We're okay! They won't hide in them houses no more, Lieutenant, we burned 'em!"

There were periods of shooting and then silence. During one of the lulls, Almeron and Susanna went to the roof. He explained, "Sue, you remember when we beat the Mexicans last winter? We discovered

General Cos had used this ramp for his artillery and cannons. Now we're using it!''

From the platform's edge she looked to the ground. There were the horse corral and stock pens below. "What's that building over there?" she asked.

"That's the hospital. See the irrigation ditch? That's how we get our water from the river. Those adobe huts on the west wall are officers' quarters. See the piles of dirt along the back wall?''

"But, Al,'' she moaned, "Those dirt platforms don't look strong!''

"True, the Alamo was never built for a fort in the first place. There are lots of weak spots even if those walls are three feet thick and twelve feet high! Besides, how can 150 men protect a place this big?'' Shaking his head he added, "Understand Travis is writing to General Houston for help. We need more men.''

Susanna was serious as she asked, "Which way is home?''

"Which home? Gonzales is about seventy miles that way,'' he pointed to the east. "San Antonio and the Musquiz home are in the west. Well, since things are quiet, for now, why don't you go outside with the baby?''

Susanna made her way down the ramp and walked out into the compound with Angelina. The others followed. The children stared at Crockett's coonskin hat, buckskinned pants, and moccasins. He stared back. A grin slowly spread over Davy's face and a devilish twinkle danced in his eyes. He grabbed his fiddle and pulled the bow across the strings. The children danced and hopped keeping time to the music.

"Dos-a-dos, do-si-do,'' yelled a voice when the

men began to swing each other arm to arm. "Swing your partners."

Suddenly an unusual screeching noise filled the air. The children stopped, their eyes were big in wonder. Around the yard the men jeered, "Come on, John McGregor, blow that bagpipe."

The children wagged their heads back and forth looking from the fiddle to the shrill instrument. The music swelled louder and louder, then faster and faster. The listeners clapped their hands harder trying to keep up with the players.

Susanna sensed a renewed spirit. She had heard many stories about the men. They came from everywhere, few made their homes in Texas. She knew in peacetime they worked at different jobs; some were lawyers, doctors, clerks, or gunsmiths. But courage and the desire for freedom had knitted them together to fight for Texas.

Travis walked to the center of the yard and raised his hand. Silence fell. "Men, Captain Dickinson's raising the only flag we have. Sorry it's the Mexican flag of 1824, but it will remind us of our promised rights and liberties that Santa Anna wants to take from us."

All eyes watched the red and green flag wave above the fort.

Davy's voice jarred their thoughts and caught their attention. "Boys! Tell ya the truth, I'm hungry! Some of you build a fire and butcher a steer. We'll have us a barbecue! You boys get water and the women can cook some beans with them hot chili peppers. Rest of ya stay at your posts. Let's get crackin'."

Davy's words filled them with a common purpose. They burst into activity.

27

Later, the evening sky grew dark with clouds. Someone yelled, "Mark my word, there's a blue norther comin'. We're gonna need lots of wood."

The women and children headed for the church. "Sue," Almeron called. "Travis sent for me. You want to come along? Ask Trinidad to watch the baby."

Susanna turned to the pretty señorita. "Would you watch her?" The girl carried the drowsy baby into bed. In the Colonel's room they saw Davy Crockett, Captain Juan Seguin, and William Travis.

"We're all here now," Travis said wearily, running his fingers through his red hair. "Men, I've called you here to decide who should take this message to Houston."

"Seems Santa Anna's closing in so you need someone who knows this country and can speak the language," Crockett said thoughtfully. "He might have to pretend he's one of Santa Anna's men to get out."

All eyes looked at Juan Seguin. He was one of San Antonio's most important citizens and had joined the fight for freedom. Other Mexican citizens and their families were inside the Alamo fighting on the side of the Texans, too. Travis protested, "But Juan's needed here. If Santa Anna sends a message it will be in Spanish; Juan would need to translate it."

"But Sir," Almeron argued. "Like Davy said, the fellow who gets out may have to talk the language. I vote for Juan."

Travis looked at Captain Seguin. "Guess they're right. Get someone to go with you."

"I don't have a horse, Colonel. I'll ask Bowie about borrowing his." He disappeared into the night.

Crockett cleared his throat. "There's a norther

comin', how 'bout my men goin' for wood? Those shacks are in the way anyhow."

"Fine," Travis nodded absent-mindedly.

Seguin reentered the headquarters room. "Señor Jim's burning with fever, but he said I could take his horse. It's raining, but my orderly, Antonio Oroche, is saddling up the horses." Travis handed him the message for General Houston. Juan placed it in his pocket. "Good-by, *amigos*." With a quick salute, Juan was gone.

"I'll see to the wood," Davy said opening the door. A sharp blast of wind filled the room. "Just what we need, a wet norther," he mumbled as he stepped into the rain.

Travis looked at the closed door and then to Susanna. "Mrs. Dickinson, thank you for your support. Your being here gives the men courage. You're a brave woman." He turned to his papers. "See you tomorrow, good night."

"Good night," Susanna replied softly. "Thank you for your kindness."

"Night, Sir," Almeron said. "Sounds like that norther's here alright." The icy wind and rain hit their faces. Almeron took her hand, "Come on, Sue." They raced to the church. The door slammed shut behind them causing the candle, burning in a clay pot, to waver and threaten to go out.

"You're wet to the bone, Sue. I'll find some wood for a fire. Get everyone into your room, they'll freeze without heat. No need having two fires when we're so short of wood. Hurry, I'll be back." He opened the door and faced the cold again.

Susanna shielded the flickering candle near the group with her body. "Come on," she whispered. She held the candle while the mothers roused the sleepy children. They silently followed Susanna into the small room. Placing the light near the side wall, she took one of Francisca's blankets for a pallet. "You'll be warmer down there." She wished for another bed as she pointed to the floor.

"I'll put this wood in the corner," Al said. "And I'll make a fire under the window. Maybe the smoke will go up and not fill the room." The fire crackled and hissed in its struggle to burn. Al fanned the blaze with his wide-brimmed hat and said softly. "In the morning the men will be hungry. It's gonna be a cold night. I'll get some water along with the bean pot and beef. Come daylight you can cook breakfast in here. The corn is in the ammunition room. Now, Sue, you get out of those wet clothes." He surveyed the room, wishing he could keep out the cold and make it more comfortable for everyone. He kissed her cheek and whispered, "Good night."

The mothers hugged their whimpering children and muttered, "Sh, *niño*, go to sleep."

Susanna's teeth chattered as she slipped into dry clothes and snuggled into bed with her child. The fire made fearsome shadows on the ceiling like faceless soldiers. She wondered if she was cold or afraid. Susanna fought the frightening questions gnawing in her heart: How could 150 men hope to defend the Alamo? Could the old walls of the church withstand an incessant barrage? She shivered in the darkness.

5

A Cold Ray of Hope February 26

Susanna wondered the next morning, how long have we been here? It seemed a lifetime, yet she knew it had only been four days. Today was Friday, would reinforcements come today?

She thought of young Colonel Travis. It was rumored he had two children, a boy and a baby girl. Where were they? Almeron often remarked that one of Travis's greatest talents was writing powerful letters, but was he a good commander? He certainly didn't have Davy's quick wit or leadership with the men. Almeron knew more about guns and Bowie could speak better Spanish. Could Travis mold his men together to fight — for Texas?

Susanna crawled out of bed and into her dry clothes. Al thought of everything, she muttered. Inside the bean pot was the beef and a knife. She placed the pot with water over the hot coals and added more wood. She went to the ammunition room for the corn. Susanna had been there before but she was alarmed to see how little gunpowder and ammunition were left.

"Good morning, Mrs. Dickinson, let me help," Señora Esparza said from the doorway. Together they took the sack of corn into the warm room. The others were awake. Trinidad hurried for the *metate*, the crude stone bowl-shaped dish and pestle used to grind the corn. The women loosened the kernels of corn and ground some for tortillas. Some kernels they dropped into the pot with chunks of meat. The cobs were stacked near the wood. They would be used for kindling the fire. Tantalizing odors soon filled the room. The children waited quietly for their breakfast. Like a mother hen with chicks, Enrique Esparza watched over the little ones.

Al opened the door. "Um, smells good; I'm hungry." He looked at the shrinking pile of wood. "You'll need wood soon. That wind is blowing hard, and it rained most of the night. The men are soaked and freezing. It's good they can take turns coming in here to eat."

Trinidad handed him a tortilla filled with hot corn and meat. Al gobbled it down hungrily. "I'll send some water. Sue, you can cook another pot of beans while we still have wood. Don't know how long our supply will last or when we can get out for more. Travis gave us orders to save our shells. We're not to shoot unless we have to."

Throughout that cold Friday the men enjoyed the hot food and cheery fire. They, in turn, shared the news and latest rumors.

"My, it is cold!" Dr. Pollard declared. "Understand Travis is writing another message asking for more help. You remember Dr. Sutherland took the first one. Albert Martin took another. The last one to Sam Houston went with Juan Seguin. Maybe reinforcements will get here today." He watched the children tossing a corncob back and forth. "They're like happy kittens with a mouse. Guess I'd better go. Thank you, ladies. That was delicious."

They learned about Jim Bowie from Green Jameson. "Jim sent word to keep fighting. Poor man. If you'll fix some food, I'll take it to him. A nice hot tortilla would do him good, like the rest of us." He took the tortillas in his hand and called, "Good-by."

Almeron brought his final report after dark. "Still no reinforcements. Looks like another cold, cloudy night. I'll check the fire later." He bent to kiss his sleeping child and patted Susanna's arm. "Good night, Sue, sleep tight."

Finally, hours later, she threw back the blanket. The pile of wood was getting low and there wasn't much water. Susanna pulled her shawl around her and, with the bucket in hand, left the room. In the darkness she inched her way along the cold, damp church wall. At the door she called softly, "Davy?" She recognized him in the pale light of dawn.

"Mornin', Ma'am. Mighty cold out here, better get back." He saw the bucket and said. "Today we're gonna finish that old well over yonder. Santa Anna's playin' games with our water ditch, but don't you worry. We'll get water. Boys will bring you some of the wood we got last night; Al said you needed some."

The wind caught the bushy tail hanging from his coonskin cap. His black hair waved around his weary face. He laughed half-heartedly. "Tell you a fact, Missus Dickinson. I hate bein' cooped up like this! Lots rather just shoot it out with them fellers. And this waitin' gets on my nerves." He rubbed his hands together for warmth. "You'd better go back before you freeze." Frowning at the thought, he called. "Say one of you fetch some wood, I'll get water. We gotta look after our women and young-uns. Oh, 'most forgot." He pulled a carved piece of wood from his pocket. "Ain't much, but I whittled it

33

for the baby. Supposed to be a dolly," he said with a grin.

Susanna wondered how he could find time to think of whittling with bullets whizzing by. "Thank you, Davy. Angie will love it." She stood on her tip-toe to kiss his leathery cheek. He blushed with pleasure. "Thanks, Davy."

"Baby, baby," Angelina cooed over her doll.

Time passed slowly. Gregorio Esparza brought the final news. "Colonel Travis is asking for help in another message to Fannin. This time the Colonel is sending James Bonham. He knows his best friend will get through to Goliad if anyone can. He told Bonham to wear a white handkerchief around his hat so the sentries will know him if he returns in the darkness."

With that ray of hope, February 27 crept to an end. Guns and cannons boomed intermittently during the long night.

6

A Lull February 28

Late the next afternoon one of the men came to the room and said, "Ladies. Wind's dyin' down and things are quiet, why don't you come listen to the music. Do us all good to laugh a little."

The children squealed in delight. The group, bundled in shawls and blankets, hurried to the compound. The little ones raced toward the music. Everyone was clapping and whistling when the song ended. "Again, again," they yelled.

Raising his hand, Crockett announced in a loud voice. "We have a special treat. Cannoneer Micajah Autry is gonna play for us."

Micajah stepped to the center. "Folks, let's sing. Guess most of you know, 'The Battle,' don't you? Words go like this:

> O watch and fight and pray;
> Our battles never over;
> Renew it boldly every day,
> Our battles never over.

I'll play it first, then we'll all sing."

The air was filled with sweet-sounding notes of heavenly music. To the ears of the listeners, Davy's hoedown fiddle had turned into a priceless violin. With the final note, a peaceful silence gripped the group. Then there was clapping and shouting.

Micajah cried, "All right, everybody join in on the words. Sing real loud, let me hear you." One by one, they opened their mouths. Deep raspy tones rang out. Each time the music stopped the men would shout, "More, more."

Davy stepped forward. "Men, give Autry a rest. This is the last Sunday in February, only right we let Preacher Garnett read to us from the Good Book." A soft moan came from someone.

Susanna didn't know much about preachers, but William Garnett sounded like a good one to her. She leaned forward to hear.

The Tennessean opened his Book. "Men, it says 'To everything there is a season . . . A time to weep, a time to laugh.' In Psalms it says:

> Yea, though I walk through the valley of the shadow of death, I will fear no evil: for thou art with me; thy rod and thy staff they comfort me . . .

He closed the Book. "Boys, I reckon this is our time to laugh, tomorrow we can weep. We gotta give our best for what we believe is right as we go through this valley. Bow your heads.

> You know why we're here and what we're tryin' to do. Help us. Give us strength. Oh, 'most forgot. Let Fannin send them reinforcements real soon. Amen."

Susanna wondered if she should laugh or cry. She heard someone mutter, "Thank you, Garnett."

Micajah drew the bow across the violin strings. A hush fell on the Texans. In a loud voice he cried. "Men, I wrote this song. Words go like this:

36

We're living for Texas
Most beautiful land I know,
We're fighting for Texas,
Most wonderful place I know.

The men bellowed out the song. When the notes faded their applause sounded like a herd of stampeding buffaloes.

The mood changed. Davy played a noisy, knee-slapping song. "There's Bowie," a man yelled. The music stopped, all heads turned. Bowie's cot was carried to the center of the compound.

Jim raised himself on one elbow and spoke in a weak voice. "Men, that music warms my heart, singing is good for the soul." A cough shook his body. "No matter what happens, boys, I beg you to keep fighting for Texas, for freedom." He collapsed in a spell of coughing. His feeble hand offered his blessings as they carried him back to his quarters.

The brief escape was over, but hope and courage had been revived. The booming of a distant cannon reminded Susanna of the red "no quarter" banner.

7

Reinforcements February 29

That Leap Year Monday seemed an eternity to Susanna. The dismal day ended as it had started — hazy with battle.

In the wee morning hours Susanna sat up with a start. A nearby rifle shot had split the darkness to awaken her. There was confusion outside. What could it mean? She had to know. Slipping into her shoes, she found her way to the church door. Peering into the night, Susanna heard the news.

"Reinforcements! They've come!"

"How many?"

"32 from Gonzales."

"Only 32? We need 200 to defend these walls!"

By the dim light Susanna could see men adding wood to the low fires. A deep voice called, "Let's celebrate! Gonna kill the fatted calf. Nothin' like roast beef and corn for a celebration party."

"Well," came an answer, "If that's the case, we've been havin' a celebration every day, that's all we've had to eat!" Laughter filled the darkness.

Susanna smiled and shook her head. They didn't need her. At three o'clock in the morning, she didn't need them or their party.

Susanna didn't feel the morning's chill, thoughts of reinforcements warmed her heart. She grabbed the bucket as she ran from the room calling, "Almeron, Almeron."

He was bubbling with excitement as he met her at the top of the ramp. "Sue, we got help! Thirty-two came from Gonzales — Albert Martin, John Smith, David Cummings, and even Galba Fuqua!"

She gasped, "Why, Galba's just a boy."

"Don't you tell him that," her husband scolded. "Understand William King came because he thought his Pa was needed at home with the nine children."

"But William's a baby!"

"Sue, if they can shoot and aren't blind, we need them!" Seeing the unhappy look on her face, he changed his tone. "I haven't talked to them, but we've heard the news from up here. Albert Martin says some English fellow wanted to help them get in last night. They couldn't recognize him in the dark, but for some reason Martin got suspicious and gave the order to shoot. The fellow disappeared into the bushes. Must of been one of Santa Anna's men leading them into a trap."

Susanna's eyes twinkled, "Oh, I'm glad that someone finally came."

"Yes, and would you believe we had our first casualty in eight days of fighting? Our sentry thought they were Mexicans and hit one of them in the foot!" Al declared in disgust. "We had a celebration after they arrived, so you go eat, Sue. I'll be down later and we'll talk to the boys. Besides, it's turned cold again. Run along now." He saw the bucket, "Ask the fellows to get you some water. Hurry, before you freeze."

Carefully picking her way down the ramp, she marveled at the difference a day had made. To know the outside world was aware of their problem was encouraging. Somehow even the morning seemed brighter in spite of the clouds.

David Cummings saw Susanna open the door. She remembered their friendly talks during the happy days when he and Davy stayed at the Musquiz home. David took the bucket and shook her hand. "Morning, Mrs. Dickinson. How's the baby? I've missed her. Can't wait to see that little Angel." His face grew serious, "You don't suppose she's forgotten me, do you?"

"Of course not, David," she laughed. "You'll see. You get some water and I'll bring her, if she's awake."

Grinning from ear to ear, Cummings turned to the nearest Tennessean. "Hey, where's the water? I'm gonna see my girl, little Angelina!"

"What do ya mean *your* girl? She's mine," was the reply.

David was waiting at the door when Susanna returned with the baby. He extended his hands. Angelina gave a squeal and wiggled into his arms. He swung her over his head and cried, "How's the prettiest little darling in Texas?" In answer she nestled contentedly against his coat.

"Ma'am," Crockett called over the loud talking from the men. "You know we've had orders to save our bullets, but Travis is going to waste a few cannon balls in celebration of reinforcements getting here."

"Yes," David interrupted, "Bowie figured maybe we could hit old Santa Anna with a couple of cannon balls."

40

Crockett went on talking, "Almeron's gonna do the shootin', you wanta watch? We'll keep the baby for you."

"Oh, yes," she called back over her shoulder, "Thank you." She darted through the church, up the ramp to her husband's side again.

"Boys," Almeron voice rang out loud and clear so all below could hear. "Fire the cannon!"

The Texans waited. The cannon boomed. One great blast and then another rumbled toward the west. Wood and rocks were hurled into the air as the balls hit a building. Pandemonium broke loose in the yard.

"Hurrah! That's showin' 'em!"

Al took Susanna's hand, "Let's go talk to the boys from home!"

They rushed like children into the yard, amid the crowd. Al shook hands and exchanged greetings with one friend after another. "What's the news from Gonzales?" he questioned.

Another asked, "What's happening out there, Kimball?"

"Fellows," the group moved closer to hear Captain George Kimball's words. "Delegates and men from all over Texas are meeting right now at Washington-on-the Brazos. We've all been talking about independence from Mexico for a long time — maybe now they'll do something about it."

"Independence?" the word echoed down the line.

"Hurrah for Texas."

"Hurrah for Independence," the Texans shouted.

Susanna thought again what a difference a day had made. If the men at the Alamo could hold off the Mexican army so other Texans could gather men, arms, supplies and strength, what a wonderful help that would be!

41

8

No Fannin March 2

Minutes and hours of the next day ticked by slowly. Yesterday's excitement over reinforcements was a memory. There was an uneasy silence over the fort. The men watched and hoped for additional help before Santa Anna closed his trap on them. They knew the Mexican troops were moving closer. In her heart, Susanna felt theirs was a battle of nerves.

MARCH 3

The women settled into a daily routine of work. They filled the water buckets, tended the fires and cooked. Yet, somehow for them life was different. They waited, always waited, but for what? Which would come first — reinforcements or Santa Anna's mighty army, some 5,000 strong? Where would it end?

The Mexican bombardment came in sudden outbursts to be followed by periods of silence. During one of the more peaceful moments Green and his engineers repaired weakened places along the wall. The men piled the dirt higher around the platforms and stomped it with their feet. They knew the next attack would destroy their efforts.

A shout from the sentry broke the stillness. "Bonham! It's Bonham! He's back!" Word spread quickly.

Almeron grabbed the baby and started for the gate. "Come on, Sue, let's hear the news."

Everyone clustered around Bonham's horse. It was white with lather. "James went straight to headquarters," Cummings told them.

"Captain Dickinson," called Joe, Travis's servant. "You're wanted in the office."

"Let's go, Sue," Almeron shouted over the excitement. Crockett, Travis, and Bonham were waiting when they entered the room. "Good to have you back, James,' Al said.

The Colonel looked at Bonham. "Let's have your report, we're all here now."

Bonham stood in the center of the room, they waited. Tired and weary from his hard ride back from Goliad and Gonzales, the captain shrugged his shoulders. "I traveled over 350 miles the last five days, but haven't much to report. Fannin's holed up in Goliad!" He looked at Travis. Friends since childhood, they knew and understood each other as men and soldiers. James flatly declared, "William, Fannin isn't coming!"

Travis blazed. "Not coming? Didn't he get my messages?"

"Yes," Bonham nodded. "Said he had started out three times, but the equipment broke down each time. They just aren't coming."

The men stared in disbelief.

In disgust, the Colonel moaned. He shook his head. "That settles it! I had about given Fannin up anyway. That's why I sent a message to Sam Houston. Other Texans can't turn their backs on us like Fannin. Sooner or later we will get help. There are over 180 of us, we will fortify the walls and wait. We have food for twenty days or so." He looked at Angelina and touched her baby cheek. "We'll stick it out, won't we?" He answered his own question. "Sure we will."

"Sh — listen," Crockett muttered. "What's that?"

They listened. A great racket came from the west. The group in the office scrambled into the open yard. Another roar filled the air. Travis called to the lookout on the gun platform above them, "What was that? Can you see anything?"

They waited for the answer, "Sir, looks like troops marching from the west. Why, looks like a thousand swarming ants marching toward the city!"

An eerie silence settled on the men. From the distance came the words, "Santa Anna! Santa Anna!" Suddenly, the church bells began to ring in San Fernando.

Susanna shuddered. Thoughts of the blood red flag above the tower blinded her vision.

Standing tall and straight, Travis ordered, "Find Scout John W. Smith for me." Regaining his confidence, he added. "Men, I'm sending out another dispatch—one to Governor Henry Smith and one to General Sam Houston. Pass the word along. The messages will go out tonight. If the men want to write their families, their letters will be sent."

In full view of all his men, the Colonel gave a snappy military salute. The sword on his belt clattered as he returned to his room.

Al's eyes were filled with concern as he said,

"Sue, we're surrounded in all directions. They'll be moving those new batteries closer." He paused for strength to say his words. "I don't want to scare you, but we're trapped! Wish you and the baby weren't here, but you are." He was choked with emotion. "No matter what happens, I want you to know I love you. You have given us courage. To the men, and me, you're the girl of the Alamo."

Tears filled her eyes. Words, for once, escaped her. She squeezed his hand.

The darkness of Thursday night fell upon the lonely fort. Sometime later a blast of musket fire shook the stillness. Susanna hugged Angelina and trembled. Sound of a lone horse's hoofs came through the window. Had James Smith gotten out with the messages from Travis and the men?

MARCH 4

The next day booming cannons drew nearer. Rifle and musket continued to bombard the fort. A sense of doom fell upon the brave band of patriots.

MARCH 5

Saturday dawned cold and clear with a north wind. All day the 180-odd Texans watched and held their fire. Ammunition was more valuable than gold. Inside the small room, the women tried to soothe the children. They were frightened from the never ending noise.

A silence fell like a lull before a storm in late afternoon of their twelfth day. A sentinel called from his station, "I see soldiers marching out of town with axes, ladders, and crowbars."

The stillness was more frightening than the

noise. Susanna and the women hurried outside, the children were right behind. Colonel Travis walked into the courtyard, too, and listened. No sound was heard. Nothing. He waited, still no shots. Silence. Travis decided to take advantage of the hush. "Men, build the fires. It is cold but for tonight we'll cook out here in the open." He looked toward the chapel. "Could you women make some tortillas? We're all hungry."

In answer to his request, *metates* and corn were quickly moved outdoors. Soon the smell of food filled the air. Everyone was hungry. They enjoyed the hot tortillas and blessed calm. Susanna boiled water for tea. With Angelina following her, she poured the hot tea into tin cups for the men. Pouring the drink, she worked her way to the west wall. She saw Travis at his desk. "Colonel," she called from the doorway. "Would you like some tea?"

"Sounds good." A gentle smile softened his worried face as he gave Susanna the cup on his desk. Angelina's baby hands tugged at his leg. He took her in his arms. Giggling happily, she hugged his neck before squirming down. Travis slipped a gold ring from his finger and tied it with a string from his pocket. "Here, little one," he called. The baby toddled toward the shiny object with outstretched hands. He slid the string necklace over her head and muttered softly, "I won't need that anymore. Keep it for me." He kissed her soft cheek and turned to Susanna. She saw his forehead was etched with lines. "Mrs. Dickinson, I'm going to talk to the men. I would like for you to hear."

They were chilled by the north wind as they stepped into the courtyard. Susanna was surprised to see Bowie's cot.

46

"Men, fall in facing the church. I have something to say." Travis's command rang loud and clear.

The women and Susanna stood in the shadows behind the Colonel. One by one the troops fell in place. They looked exhausted.

Travis cleared his throat and began. "We haven't lost a man, not one has been wounded in battle. We've been lucky." Looking from face to face, Travis was suddenly overcome with emotion. He coughed nervously. "I believed for days that we'd get reinforcements enough to defend this fort and be able to turn back the enemy. Now," he took a deep breath. "I know no more help is coming. It could never get here in time. Not now."

They stood in hushed silence. Colonel Travis announced, "I think you should know we have three choices. We could surrender." He stopped. Thoughts of the red flag waved before Susanna's eyes. "You could try to escape." She knew they were visualizing the troops around the fort. "Or — we can fight to the end!" Finally, Susanna thought, the dreaded truth is out!

The men were statues, thinking their own thoughts. Travis had spoken the truth. However, he had neglected to add there was no choice — "Victory or Death."

Standing tall and straight, his red hair glistening in the fading light, Travis continued. "Any delay here may slow Santa Anna's progress and advancement to give General Houston time to gather troops to fight for Texas. So . . . for me . . . there is no question — I shall never surrender or retreat!"

Unsheathing the sword that always hung at his side, Travis walked in front of the men. On the ground he drew a line. Replacing the sword he said,

"Each of you is free to make a choice. If you are willing to stay here and die with me, step over this line." He backed into the shadows.

Susanna shuddered. Travis's meaning was clear. He was not asking for life but for death! Tapley Holland was the first to cross the line. Man after man followed, too fast to count. Only two remained behind.

"Men," Jim Bowie yelled from his bed. "Help me. Carry me across." Those nearest rushed to obey his request. Susanna's heart overflowed with pride and fear. Everyone stared at the lone man — Louis "Moses" Rose.

"Rose," Davy boomed. "There's no way to escape. You've told us how you fought with Napoleon in that Russian war, but you've never fought this Napoleon of the West. Santa Anna will never let you go!"

Bowie cried, "Louis Rose, we've been friends for years. You know I wouldn't tell you wrong. Think what you're doing. You'll never get to Nacogdoches — not now, not over that wall."

A hush fell upon the men. Rose was determined. "I'll get away. I have fought many battles but I'm not ready to die here." All eyes watched him take his bundle, scale the wall and disappear.

Travis spoke, "Men, the enemy could attack at any time. For now, go back to your posts and get some sleep. Some of you take Dickinson's and Esparza's places and others, if there are any with families. Let them be together." His voice faltered. "Thank you and some day, men, Texas will thank you. You're dismissed."

Struggling with her tears, Susanna whispered, "Colonel. Thank you. You are a brave man." She looked at the gallant Texans. What could she say?

48

There were no words to express the feelings or emotions welled up inside. Her eyes met Davy's.

"Good night, Ma'am."

She could not answer. She turned to escape the overpowering gloom that swept her soul.

9

The Battle March 6, 5 A.M.

The earth trembled with a thud. Blaring bugles gave the signal to advance. Marching feet and beating drums rumbled in the darkness.

"*Viva Santa Anna!*" "*Arriba!*" floated on the air, followed by "The Mexicans are coming!" Travis's command was loud, "Give them hell!"

"They're coming," Susanna cried. She raced with Angelina in her arms to the adjoining room. Muffled screams and wails from her friends added to her fears. On the floor they crouched over the children to protect them from oncoming danger.

The room was filled with momentary brightness from rockets. Enrique Esparza dashed to the window and heard the bugle notes. "Oh, mama, *deguello,* no quarter," he moaned.

Distant drums rolled their deadly dirge. Smoke from bullets and gunpowder quickly filled the early dawn. The door of their room flew open. Susanna stared at sixteen-year-old Galba Fuqua. A bullet had broken his jaw. Unable to speak, he turned in despair to return to his comrades. Sobs mingled with prayers as the women huddled closer.

Travis was manning a cannon when the first attack hit the north wall. Shotgun in hand, he fired down at the ladder where Mexicans were scaling the wall. His bayonet was raised high when he reeled and fell. Dead. A single bullet had pierced his forehead.

A steady bombardment hit the crumbling walls. Finally, an ear-splitting crash broke the last barrier. The enemy swarmed in and headed for the low barracks. Jim Bowie lay with pistols cocked and his knife at his side. Santa Anna's men pushed forward. Jim fired. His bullets hit their mark. One soldier crumbled and the other fell across his bed. A Mexican rifle blazed. A peaceful smile softened his pale dead face. The enemy turned to the Texans along the wall.

Would it never end, Susanna wondered. Suddenly, Al ran into the room. "Sue," he cried, "the Mexicans are inside the walls. If they spare you, save our child! I love you." With one quick embrace, he was gone.

She saw the gruesome battle. Crockett and his men fired, loaded, and fired again. Down, one by one, they went — Mexican over Texan, blending in a heap. With a final plunge, Davy's bayonet pierced his attacker. He fell. The coonskin cap dropped beside his faithful rifle. The hero was dead.

Bayonet fought rifle butt, there was no time to reload. More soldiers pushed over the walls, outnumbering the Texans by staggering odds. Shells disintegrated the church doors. Santa Anna's men raced into the chapel firing in all directions. Crazed with the sight of blood, Mexican shot Mexican in the confusion. Up the ramp they surged. Jim Bonham, bayonet raised, fell on his victim. Dead.

"Jim." Al's voice was stopped. His body covered his trusty cannon. Santa Anna's mighty force turned to the smaller rooms. Shrill screams drowned the deadly noises. Gregorio Esparza was killed at the door. His family watched him fall. With a flaming torch in one hand, Robert Evans crawled toward the powder room. A bullet erased Evan's dreams of blowing up the ammunition.

Jacob Walker ran into the room, followed by four soldiers. Deafening sounds of bullets rocked the small room. Unable to scream, Susanna shook in fright. Too numbed to move, she clasped her child tightly. The room reeled. She felt Jacob's fingers touch her foot. His limp body fell at her side. Susanna collapsed over her baby.

10

Santa Anna March 6, 8 A.M.

Death had stilled the Texans' guns in the ninety minute battle. The sun's first rays shimmered over the pools of blood beside the lifeless bodies of Mexicans and Texans, as the haze settled over the shattered but heroic Alamo.

Stunned and dazed, Susanna sat on the floor. A shadow filled the doorway. "Is Mrs. Dickinson here?" She could not speak. "Is there a Mrs. Dickinson here?" The voice spoke in perfect English.

Slowly Susanna raised her head, she stared at the Mexican officer. Too limp to answer, she nodded her head. "I am General Manuel Castrillon. If you value your life, speak up. Follow me."

Susanna struggled to her feet, clinging to her child. She stumbled behind the colorful uniform. Avoiding the fallen logs from the overhead ramp, they neared the gaping hole where a door had been.

Suddenly, from the shadows, an ugly face leered at Susanna. He grabbed her arm with blood-stained hands. She screamed.

Sword in hand, the General threatened. "Stop! Santa Anna has need of her." The blood-crazed soldier sank back against the wall.

Walking into the courtyard, Susanna felt a sharp pain in her leg. As she lurched forward, the

General grabbed her arm to prevent her falling. "Señora?"

Clutching her child, she lifted the hem of her long dress with her right hand. Blood oozed from a bullet hole in the calf of her leg. The officer glared angrily at the Mexicans around them and clasped her arm protectively. With the tip of his sword, he commanded the nearest men. "Help her." The soldiers helped her toward the long barracks. The General carried her child.

Suddenly, Susanna gasped, and tears filled her eyes. On the ground at their feet lay the body of David Crockett. Then she saw his rifle and coonskin cap. Blinded by memories of his smile she heard his Tennessee drawl, "Mornin', Ma'am."

Death's peace filled her soul. Emotionless, too tired to feel, she looked from body to body. She knew them all: James Garrett, John McGregor, William Mills, Jacob Darst. Row on row of lifeless faces floated before her eyes like a roll call in the sky. The Mexican soldiers helped her as they followed the General out of the silent fort. Susanna saw the red banner still fluttering in the early dawn.

The hours that followed were like a dream. She had no memory of her leg being treated. Susanna found herself holding her child and a cup of coffee. She blinked and stared at the gold epaulet insignia on the broad shoulders in front of her. She whispered, "Santa Anna."

"Si, Señora. General Antonio Lopez de Santa Anna, President of Mexico — and Texas."

With spotless white gloves he took Angelina onto his lap. "*Hermosa, muy hermosa.* What a beautiful child." The baby played with the brightly ribboned medals that covered the chest of his dazzling uniform. Leaning his handsome face nearer to Angelina's, her dimpled fingers stroked his graying temples. Susanna could tell his cold, cruel heart was melting.

"Señora, I want this child." He touched the baby's soft cheek. "I will give her everything — clothes, jewels, a good education — the best of Mexico will be hers."

Susanna shrieked in horror, "Never!"

A frown creased his forehead. "Señora, you do not understand. You will go with her. You, too, will have the best. Instead of those rags, I will give you silks. You will be beautiful." His eyes sparkled at the thought. "You will be a girl again." Smugly, thinking she could not resist his charms, he waited.

Susanna straightened. With pride filled eyes, she took her child. "General, it is you who does not understand. My husband and those brave friends died for Texas and I belong to Texas — Texas and freedom. So does my child." Her voice was proud and firm.

Santa Anna's face reddened with anger. He glared at Susanna and spit the word. *"Estúpido."* He stood to his feet. "Very well, Señora, you will pay the price! When your leg is better you will take my message to your Texans. I will send my servant, Ben, as an escort. You will go to Sam Houston to warn that further resistance will be useless. I will give 'no quarter.' "

He turned to General Castrillon and gave the command. "Identify the Texans called Travis, Bowie, and Crockett. Be sure they are dead." He paused, remembering his 600 dead and wounded. "Gather and bury our brave fighters. Then the enemy," he stopped. "The enemy you will pile in heaps and burn this day." With contempt he shouted the words, "The traitors!"

With one last glance toward Susanna, he muttered softly, "*Hermosa.*" He swaggered from the room proudly.

11

"Remember the Alamo"

Susanna looked out the window, a black cloud rose over the lonely fort. Glowing flames covered the March sky. Visions of Al's lifeless body flashed before her. "What is it?" she muttered. Then she knew. The funeral pyres were burning! Santa Anna's final blow! Now she understood the meaning of "no quarter." Drums rolled their final cadence for the heroes. Realization of the awful scene hit Susanna, she sank upon the cold floor.

A thin veil suspended her between heaven and hell. She floated through the long hours that followed. Deadened by shock and heartache, Susanna cared little about her world. She was feverish, her throbbing leg matched the pain in her heart.

Sometime later Susanna realized she and her child were placed upon a horse. "Mrs. Dickinson." That voice brought her to reality. She trembled. Santa Anna called her name again. "Mrs. Dickinson." Looking down she fought the hatred that surged over her. His face was serious as he handed her the letter. "Take this to Sam Houston. You will be safe, my soldiers will escort you beyond our lines.

My servant, Ben, will go with you to Gonzales and the General." Tenderly for only her ears, he spoke. "Señora, I would care for you and your baby." She could not answer.

Filing past Santa Anna, the small group of riders headed slowly into the rising sun. Susanna took one painful look back to the battle-scarred shell of the Alamo etched against the Texas sky. A sob escaped her lips. By the pale morning light the crumbling church was a grim reminder of those thirteen days.

Mile after mile they traveled, and Susanna's thoughts were far away. She never knew, or cared, when the three Mexican soldiers turned back. Her horse followed Ben's pony over the narrow trail.

Hours later they crossed Salado Creek to find the path on the opposite bank. Suddenly, sensing danger, the horses flattened their ears. She saw weeds moving near her foot. Susanna gasped. Someone was hiding there. Peering into the undergrowth, she glimpsed the familiar face of Colonel Travis's servant. She gave a sigh of relief. "Joe," she cried, "You scared me half to death."

The Negro's happy face appeared from the bushes. "You are real, I thought you were dead, Mrs. Dickinson!"

"Of course I'm real," Susanna replied. "What are you doing here? Did Santa Anna let you go?"

The Negro's face glistened. "He said I could go and go I did." Casting a fearful glance behind him, he groaned. "But he might change his mind. Can I walk 'long behind you? I won't be no trouble."

"Come on," she nodded. "Ben's leading our way. We're going to Sam Houston."

Joe trailed after the two riders. They moved in

silence. Later Ben slowed his pony closer to Susanna's. He pointed to the trail ahead. Two horsemen were riding in their direction.

Joe's voice trembled, "Indians?"

"If they are," Susanna declared firmly, "We'll meet them head on. I'm not hiding anymore."

As the riders neared, Ben laughed. "They're not Indians, they're Texans!"

They neared the riders. Susanna lifted her hand in greeting and declared, "I'm Mrs. Almeron Dickinson. This is Ben, that's Joe. We are going to General Houston with a message from Santa Anna." She hesitated, gathering strength to add the words, "The Alamo has fallen!"

"Fallen?" they echoed. Susanna nodded.

"Ma'am, my name's Henry Karnes," the red head said. "That's Erastus Smith."

The older man explained. "Folks call me 'Deaf' but I ain't. That's my nickname." He clutched his battered hat. "Henry, I'll ride with them. You give the General the news. Tell him we'll be along."

Henry wheeled his horse around and headed for Gonzales. 'Deaf' Smith looked at Susanna.

"I know you're tired, Mrs. Dickinson. I've got four younguns of my own. Let me take your baby and rest you a spell." Angelina went into his outstretched arms and nuzzled contentedly against his soft deerskin jacket. "Tell me what happened, Ma'am, if you can."

Susanna told her story. When she finished her face was wet with tears. Gloom and sadness filled 'Deaf's' heart, too, as he listened. One by one he asked about his friends: David Cummings, Albert Martin, Amos Pollard — she shook her head. Dead, all were dead. Misty-eyed, 'Deaf' thought of the wives and children left by the fallen heroes. His heart was full of sadness.

EVENING OF MARCH 13

They rode in the hushed silence through the misty darkness. Rumors of the Fall of the Alamo swept the countryside like wildfire. The people of Gonzales were filled with panic. They piled their possessions on wagons and oxcarts and joined General Houston's camp. Clustering around the fires near the soldiers, they wondered their fate.

General Sam Houston was waiting to help Susanna from her horse. Stumbling with fatigue and sorrow against his arm, she sank upon the ground in front of the bright fire. 'Deaf' Smith rocked the sleeping child in his arms and waited for her to tell her story.

Holding a cup of steaming coffee, Susanna again told of the heroic battle from beginning to end. Tears of grief washed away her bitterness and hate. Handing Houston the message from Santa Anna, Susanna knew her mission was complete. She took Angelina and clutched her to her breast.

Patting Susanna's arm, the General said, "You're a brave woman. Mrs. Dickinson, this is Lieutenant Arcelus Dodson. He's in charge of the women and children running away from Santa Anna. He'll take care of you." Houston's head was low in sorrow as he turned to his soldiers.

The tall bearded Lieutenant helped Susanna to her feet. Susanna took her horse's reins and looked at the man. "I sure could use a horse," he said. General Houston gave orders to burn Gonzales. Understand a blind woman's been left behind. If I had a horse I could go for her.

"Oh, Isaac Millsap's wife and seven children!" She handed him the reins. "Here, please take my horse."

They neared the group huddled by the fire. Susanna stared from one widow's tear-streaked face to another. They crowded round for news of their husbands and sons. What could she say?

From out of the darkness a whining shadow crept up to her feet. Susanna gasped in disbelief. "J.B. — you found me!" His wagging tail and soft cry gave his answer. With Angelina and the dog in her arms, memories of Almeron flooded her being.

Susanna looked up. For one brief moment the clouds parted, the heavens seemed aglow with many new stars. Never had they seemed so bright.

An inner quiet soothed her heart. She heard the words:

Yea, though I walk through the valley of the shadow of death, I will fear no evil . . .

The walk "through the valley" had bathed her in peace. No longer afraid, she could face tomorrow. Sam Houston could now unfurl the banner of freedom over Texas with the cry, "Remember the Alamo."

Epilogue

Susanna Dickinson, like the other widows of the Texas Revolution, faced many hardships in the years that followed. Her daughter, Angelina, died at the age of thirty-five, leaving two children for her mother to raise. Susanna lived for some years in Houston, and later moved to Austin, the capital of Texas. She died there on October 7, 1883, at the age of sixty-eight. She was buried in Oakwood Cemetery.

As the only adult Anglo-American to survive the Fall of the Alamo, she was required many times over the years to give her account of the battle. Without her story many of the details would have been unknown. Susanna Dickinson will forever remain in history *Girl of the Alamo.*

Susannah Dickenson, wife of Alamo defender, Almeron Dick-
enson. Photo taken years after the Alamo battle.
— Courtesy Archives Division, Texas State Library

Angelina Dickenson, daughter of Almeron and Susannah Dickenson, a child survivor of the Alamo battle. Photo taken years after the Alamo battle.

— Courtesy Prints and Photographs Collection, Barker Texas History Center, University of Texas at Austin

Bibliography

JUVENILE

Driskill, Frank, *Davy Crockett, the Untold Story,* Eakin Publ., Burnet, Texas, 1981

Flynn, Jean, *Jim Bowie, A Texas Legend,* Eakin Publ., Burnet, Texas, 1980

Johnson, William, *The Birth of Texas,* Houghton Mifflin, Boston, 1960

Maher, Ramona, *Their Shining Hour,* John Day Co., New York, 1960

Laycock, George and Ellen, *How the Settlers Lived,* McKay Co., New York, 1980

ADULT

Habig, Marion, *The Alamo Mission,* Franciscan Herald Press, Chicago, 1977

King, Richard, *Susanna Dickinson: Messenger of the Alamo,* Shoal Creek, Austin, Texas 1976

Lord, Walter, *A Time to Stand,* University of Nebraska Press, Lincoln, 1961

Myers, John, *The Alamo,* University of Nebraska Press, Lincoln, 1948

Nevin, David, *The Texans,* Time-Life Books, New York, 1975

Potter, Reuben, *The Fall of the Alamo,* Otterden Press, Hillsdale, New Jersey, 1977

Sheffy, Lester, *Texas,* Banks Upshaw and Company, Dallas, 1954

Tinkle, Lon, *The Alamo, 13 Days of Glory,* New American Library, Signet, New York, 1958

MAGAZINE AND PERIODICAL ARTICLES

Texas Parade, January 1956, "Lady of the Alamo"

Texas Parade, January 1964, "Susanna Dickinson, the Alamo's Forgotten Heroine" by Curtis Bishop

Texas magazine, "The Heroine of the Alamo" by R. Shuffler

A. M. Wright, "Abstract of Biographical Data in Texas Supreme Court Reports" M.A. thesis. University of Texas

The West, "The Alamo's Messenger of Defeat" by L. C. Auer

Austin News, "The Alamo's Mrs. Dickinson Dies at Age 68 in Austin"